HOW TO REGISTER TO VOTE

HOW TO DO YOUR PART TO PROTECT THE FUTURE OF DEMOCRACY

ROBERT FOWLER

Green
Butterfly
Press

CONTENTS

INTRODUCTION

How to Use This Book

This book provides you with all of the general guidelines for registering to vote, as well as information about voting in general. Most states follow mostly the same or similar rules. That said, it's important to know if your state has any unique rules or procedures. We've included some state-specific information in this book, but the information changes frequently and it's always a good idea to call or check online for any information or updates specific to your location.

For that reason, in the State Information chapter (Chapter 3), you'll find a listing of the voting information phone numbers and websites for all U.S. states, territories, and the District of Columbia. After reading this book, be sure to get any outstanding questions answered there, as well as taking advantage of any online voter-related services that may be available in your state.

ONE

HOW TO REGISTER TO VOTE

Are You Ready to Vote?

Congratulations on your decision to exercise your constitutional right to participate in democracy. Voting is not only a right, but it's also exciting! When you vote, you're literally standing up and being counted, making your voice heard as a citizen.

Voting is simple, too. But first, are you eligible to vote in the United States of America? Let's find out!

Eligibility: 3 Basic Requirements

Are you eligible to vote? There are three main requirements you must meet in order to vote in the United States:

1. You must be a United States citizen.
2. You must meet your state's requirements for residency. Note: you can be homeless and still meet these state requirements. Check your state (Chapter 3) for details.

3. You must be 18 years old on or before election day.

In some states, you can register to vote before you turn 18 if you will be 18 by election day. If this applies to you, visit your state's voting website for details (see Chapter 3).

Some states allow 17-year-olds to vote in primaries* if the voter will be 18 by the time of the general election. For details, see:

http://www.fairvote.org/primary_voting_at_age_17#facts_17_year_old_primary_voting

* Note on terminology: Primary elections, or "primaries," are special elections to select each political party's candidate for the regular election, which is called the "general" election.

If you meet these three criteria, then you can probably vote! (There are some rare exceptions, described below.)

But remember, each state runs federal and state elections in their own way. Your state and local election offices will have the exact rules for voting in your state. To avoid any problems, be sure to check those specific details in your state (see Chapter 3).

North Dakota Residents

Did you know that all states require you to register before you can vote, except one? The exception: North Dakota. If you live in North Dakota, you don't need to register.

Who Cannot Vote

Some people cannot vote. Are you one of them? Here are groups of people who cannot vote in U.S. elections:

- Non-citizens, including permanent legal residents, cannot vote.
- Individuals with felony convictions may or may not be allowed to vote, depending on the state. Check with the elections office for your state about the laws where you reside (see Chapter 3).
- Some people who are mentally incapacitated cannot vote. Again, these rules vary by state.

Voter Registration Deadlines

Most states have registration deadlines, meaning that you must register some time prior to the election, such as 30 days. The time period varies by state. See the State Information in Chapter 3 for details on your state.

Same Day Registration

As of March 2018, 17 states and the District of Columbia allow you to register on the same day you vote. See the State Information in Chapter 3 for details on your state.

Voter Registration Cards

If you've recently turned in a voter registration application or changed your voter registration, it may take a few weeks for your new voter registration card to arrive in the mail.

Voting Registration Options

No matter where you live, you have some options for registering to vote.

Registering Online or In-Person

Notice: FIRST TIMERS: If it's your first time registering to vote, there are some things to consider.

If you are voting for the first time in your state and you're submitting a voter registration form through the mail, then you may be required to show proof of identification the first time you go to vote. Requirements vary by state, but proof of identification could be a current and valid photo identification OR a current utility bill, bank statement, government check, paycheck or some form of government document that shows your name and address.

However, you may not be required to show proof of identification at the polling place (or when voting by mail) if:

- You provided copies of the above (proof of identification) with your voter registration form
- Your voter registration form has been verified by an election official
- You're entitled by Federal law to vote by absentee ballot
- Your state or local election official matched the driver's license number or social security information on your application with a Federal or State identification record bearing the same number, name, and date of birth.

Again, please note that individual states may have additional voter identification requirements so be sure to check! Moreover, if you met the Federal proof-of identification requirement when you registered, some states may also require identification at the polling place.

Online Registration

Perhaps the easiest way to register to vote is to register online. As of March 2018, online registration was available for 37 states plus the District of Columbia and Guam. See the State Information section to see if your state offers online registration.

There are two ways to register online:

1. Register using your state's website, if online registration functionality is available (see the State Information section), or
2. Download a National Mail Voter Registration Form (NMVRF) from the U.S. Election Assistance Commission (EAC) web site.

The NMVRF process is simple. Visit http://www.eac.gov/NVRA, select your language, state, and download the .PDF form (or open it in your browser).

If you need help, call (866)747–1471. You can also find NMVRF and State voter registration forms at your local library, public schools, and city and county clerk offices.

If you downloaded the .PDF form, print it out, fill it out by hand, sign it, and mail it to the address for your state, which is provided in the form's instructions.

If you opened the .PDF form in your browser, you can fill it out on-screen. When you're finished, print it out, sign it, and mail it in.

Whichever method you use, *don't forget to sign the form!*

The NMVRF has a helpful "State Instructions" section that lists the requirements for each State.

Note: As of this writing, North Dakota, Wyoming, and the U.S. territories American Samoa, Guam, Puerto Rico, and the U.S. Virgin Islands **do not accept** the National Mail Voter Registration Form (NMVRF). Further, New Hampshire only accepts the form as a request for a state absentee voter mail-in registration form.

Languages

The National Mail Voter Registration Form is available in several languages: English, Spanish, Chinese, Japanese, Korean, Tagalog, Vietnamese, Hindi, Bengali, and Khmer.

Voter's guides, which include information on registering to vote, can be found translated into Spanish, Chinese, Cherokee, Dakota, Japanese, Korean, Navajo, Tagalog, Vietnamese, and Yupik. Also know that the U.S. Election Assistance Commission provides information for voters on its web site in Chinese, Japanese, Korean, Spanish, Tagalog and Vietnamese. The Commission offers comprehensive glossaries of voting terms in these six languages to assist voters and election officials.

In-Person Voter Registration

If you prefer, you may alternately register in person at your state or local election office and some other government offices. Some nearby public facilities that might be an option include:

- The DMV (department of motor vehicles)
- State or local election offices
- Armed services recruitment centers
- State and county public assistance offices/agencies (state funded programs serving people with disabilities, SNAP/food stamps, WIC) - at these places you can fill out and submit a National Mail Voter Registration Form.
- A state-designated public facility established as a voter registration agency (for example: a public library, public school, and city or county clerk's office).

Confirming Your Voter Registration Information

It's a good idea to confirm that your registration information was received and that your information is correct. Every state has different ways to keep voter registrations up-to-date. Moreover, some states ***purge inactive voters from the rolls***.

When you check ahead of time to ensure that you are still properly registered to vote, you'll know if your name, address and party affiliation are up-to-date. It's recommended that you do this at least 7 weeks before an election. Inquiring this far in advance of the registration deadline gives you plenty of time to re-register, if it's needed. You'll prevent your name from accidentally being purged from your state's list of eligible voters. You'll know that you're still eligible to vote, and that you're voting at the correct polling location. If your election office removes your registration in error and you don't discover this before you go to vote, you may have to cast a provisional ballot. Furthermore, the Federal law ensures states provide an "access system" allowing you to check your provisional ballot status.

Homeless Citizens

Homeless citizens are eligible to vote in all 50 states. If registering as a homeless individual, election officials recommend listing a shelter address as the voting address where you could receive mail. Alternatively, homeless registrants can list a street corner or a park as their residence. In fact, the federal voter registration form and many state forms will have a space for this very purpose.

Updating Your Voter Registration

If you've changed your name or moved permanently, then you should re-register or update your voter registration information. It's easy to do. Depending on your state's rules, you might be able to change your registration information online, via phone, or by mail. Simply contact your state (see Chapter 13) or the "Can I Vote?" website created by the National Association of Secretaries of State (NASS):

https://www.nass.org/can-i-vote

It's also possible that your state may require you to register to vote again to change your information.

Military and Overseas Voter Registration

If you are in the military or an overseas citizen, then you can use the Federal Post Card Application (FPCA). This is available from the Federal Voting Assistance Program's (FVAP) website (fvap.gov). All states and territories accept the FPCA as an application for both registration and an absentee ballot. Printed copies of the form are also available at U.S. military bases, embassies, and consular offices. If you have questions or need more information about registering to vote or voting with an absentee ballot, contact FVAP by calling (800)438-8683, sending an email to vote@fvap.ncr.gov, or visiting fvap.gov.

TWO

HOW TO VOTE

Once you've registered to vote, you have some choices as to how you actually vote. It's important to understand that, in the United States, federal and state elections are run by the states themselves. The laws and procedures vary from state to state, so you need to know the rules for your state.

Polling Locations

Most states assign a specific "polling place" or "voting location" for each person. (A few states have ballot drop sites instead.) If you go to the wrong location, your name won't be on the roll, so it's a good idea to find out which polling place you're assigned to before election day. You'll want to know the location, as well as what time the polls open and close, so you can plan your day accordingly.

All-Mail Voting, Early Voting, and Absentee Voting

Most states provide some way for people to vote prior to Election

Day, including early voting, absentee voting (some states require an excuse, others do not), or mailing ballots to everyone.

All-Mail Voting

As of this writing, three states (WA, OR, CO) automatically mail a ballot to all registered voters. No request is necessary. (Some additional states offer All-Mail Voting for certain elections only.)

Early Voting

As of this writing, 37 states allow what's known as "early voting." This means they let voters cast their ballot before Election Day. No excuse is required. This can be convenient for many people, such as:

- those who travel and will be out of town on election day
- those who cannot leave their jobs or children to go vote
- individuals who have physical or transportation difficulties
- rural voters who live far from a ballot location
- anybody who would rather not stand in line at the ballot

Early voters can cast their vote by mail or in person at their local election official's office. Early voting dates and times vary among states. See State Information in Chapter 3 for details.

Absentee Voting

Absentee voting gives you the opportunity to vote if you're away from home during elections. This could apply to voters who:

- Live out of the country (including members of the military and military family members who are stationed overseas)
- Have a disability or injury limiting mobility
- Business travelers
- Are attending college out of state.

All states send absentee ballots to eligible voters who ask to receive one. Twenty states require excuses; the other states do not. Absentee ballots may be returned via mail or in person. Some states will automatically place you on a permanent absentee voter list for subsequent elections, from which you must request to be removed. Absentee ballot deadlines also vary from state to state. Check with your state (Chapter 3) for details about absentee voting.

If you need to vote absentee, contact your state or local election office right away to make sure you don't miss the deadline for requesting and returning an absentee ballot. If you have questions about absentee voting, in addition to contacting your state's election office, you can also contact the Federal Voting Assistance Program (FVAP) at (800)438–8683 or e-mail at vote@fvap.ncr.gov.

Identification

Depending on your state's laws, you may not need your physical voter registration card to vote, but you may need other identification. The identification may or may not be required to be a government-issued photo I.D. card. Requirements vary by state. Check your state's voter website (Chapter 3) for details.

Possible Problems on Election Day

The following could present problems when voting. Most of them are easily avoided by taking steps before Election Day to ensure that everything is in order before you head to the polls.

- If you don't have the type of voter ID required in your state. Check your state's voter website (Chapter 3).
- If you've changed your name or permanent address and you haven't updated your voter registration.
- If the name or address on your ID doesn't match the information on your voter registration.

- If you go to vote at a polling place that is not your assigned polling location.

If any of these problems arise, you might need to cast your vote as a provisional ballot.

Provisional Ballots

If you do not have the proper identification at the polling place, or if your name is not on the roll for some reason, you are eligible to cast a "provisional ballot". A provisional ballot simply means that your vote is recorded but will not count toward the election until your eligibility to vote has been verified, usually the following day.

Do I Have to Vote Along Party Lines?

When you register to vote, you don't have to join a political party or reveal your party preference. In fact, not every state accepts or lists a party affiliation on a voter registration card. On Election Day, you do not have to vote for any candidate based on the party affiliation that you might have chosen. For example, if you're a registered Republican, you can vote for a Democratic candidate, and vice versa. In general elections (as opposed to primaries), you can vote for any candidate, of any party.

Your party affiliation is generally only important for primary elections because many states have what are called "closed" primaries. This means that you can only choose to vote from among your party's candidates during the primary election. This is to let members of the party select which candidate to run for their party in the general election. Independent voters in states with closed primaries may wish to check their state's laws to see how their state handles independent voters. Some may wish to register with a party affiliation, if only to have a vote in the primaries.

Do Your Homework in Advance

Before voting day, it's a good idea to acquaint yourself with with the candidates and initiatives/propositions that will be on the ballot.

Don't wait until the last minute to do your research, as some ballot initiatives are confusing and sound like they do one thing, when they actually do something else. Sadly, some ballot initiatives are designed by special interest groups specifically to mislead voters. For example, a proposition in Arizona that purported to raise money for public schools (sounds great, right?) was actually a scheme initiated by real estate developers to trick voters into selling the state's land in nature preserves to... guess who?... real estate developers.

It's true, the proceeds from the land sales would go to the schools – so it wasn't exactly a lie – but voters who didn't hear both sides of the issue were easily duped. The sale of nature preserve lands was vastly unpopular (virtually everybody was against it except those who stood to make money), but environmentalists with good intentions nevertheless voted for the land sale because they didn't do their homework and they thought they were simply voting to give the schools more money. Don't let this happen to you – do your homework ahead of time. You don't want to be trying to figure this out in the polling booth, and it causes other voters to wait longer in line.

So how do you do your homework? States publish booklets prior to elections describing the propositions and listing public arguments both "for" and "against." By reading these arguments, it's usually easy to figure out what's really going on. You might receive a booklet in the mail. If not, you can visit your state's election website (Chapter 3) and download or read the same information online.

Voters with Disabilities

Voters with disabilities are guaranteed assistance at the polls by law. Under Federal law, if you require help to vote for reasons such as blindness, disability, or inability to read or write, you may be able to bring someone with you to help, such as a friend or relative. Polling places are equipped to accommodate the needs of voters with disabilities by providing clearly marked parking spaces, accessible entrances and ramps, and well-marked routes pointing the way to voting locations.

Before election day, it's smart to familiarize yourself with the voting device used in your jurisdiction. Learn how the device is accessible to voters with disabilities. In fact, some states even offer "curbside voting" for voters who cannot easily leave their cars. For curbside voting, a poll worker will bring all necessary materials, including a ballot, to the voter's car. Be sure to verify with your state or local election office if curbside voting is available in your jurisdiction.

Polling places also have voting equipment that makes sure every single voter is given the same opportunity for access, participation, privacy, and independence. If you have questions about the accessibility of your polling place, or need information about voting equipment for individuals with disabilities, contact your state (Chapter 3) or local election office.

Language Barriers

Voters with language barriers can get help understanding the ballot if they have a limited ability to read, speak, write, or understand English. Some of these assistance efforts are provided voluntarily by states; others are required by Federal law. This assistance can come in different forms. For example, language assistance may mean equipping polling places with ballots and voting instructions in multiple languages. Or, they might staff polling locations with bilingual poll workers. Lastly, they might provide voting information online in languages other than English. Contact your state (Chapter 3) or local election office to discover language assistance options in your area.

Voter Complaints and Voting Fraud

Voting is supposed to be a peaceful process. The integrity of our system rests on the shoulders of everyone to ensure it's a smooth and fair process. Therefore, it's vital to report any problems you might have with voting or the polling location.

If you experience a problem at a polling place or with voting procedures in your jurisdiction, please report it. You'll need to contact your state or local election office to get the proper rules for proceeding. Again, if you have problems voting, you need to report them!

If you have a problem with ballot access, including voter discrimination, immediately call the Voting Section at (800)253–3931. (The Voting Section is a department of Civil Rights Division of the U.S. Department of Justice.)

If you need to report problems related to voting fraud or voter intimidation, immediately call the department's main switchboard at (202)514–2000 or (800)253–3931 to be directed to the correct federal law enforcement agency, and they will help you. You can call the nearest office of the Federal Bureau of Investigation or your local U.S. Attorney's Office.

You can email U.S. Department of Justice using the following contact form on their website:

https://www.justice.gov/doj/webform/your-message-department-justice

Or visit the home page of the U.S. Department of Justice website:

http://usdoj.gov

Become a Poll Worker!

Want to get involved in ensuring fair and accurate elections? Poll workers are important people! They help ensure smooth, fair and accurate elections. The tasks include: preparing the precinct by setting up voting equipment, helping voters with instructions or demonstrations when using voting equipment if needed, greeting voters, verifying registrations, providing voting assistance if necessary, and providing voters with appropriate ballots. When voting ends for the day, the poll workers close the precinct and prepare election materials for delivery to the elections office.

If you want to be a poll worker, you usually need to be registered to vote in the precinct or county you want to serve. However, some states let university and college students work at polls near their school even though they might not be registered to vote in that jurisdiction. If you want to learn more about how to be a poll worker, please contact your state or local election office.

THREE

STATE INFORMATION

As mentioned previously, rules for voting and registering to vote vary by state. Because states' rules change frequently, information provided below may not be correct by the time you read this. We always recommend contacting your state official's office (or visiting its website), to make sure you have the latest information.

ALABAMA

(800)274–8683

https://sos.alabama.gov/alabama-votes

Early voting: No. Excuse required for absentee.

Same day registration: No.

Registration deadline (as of Aug 2018): 15 days prior to election.

Online registration:

https://www.alabamainteractive.org/sos/voter_registration/voterRegistrationWelcome.action

ALASKA

(907)465–4611

http://www.elections.alaska.gov

Early voting: Yes. Absentee requires no excuse.

Same day registration: No.

Registration deadline (as of Aug 2018): 30 days prior to election.

Online registration:

https://voterregistration.alaska.gov/

AMERICAN SAMOA

(684)699–3570

http://www.americansamoaelectionoffice.org

Early voting: No. Excuse required for absentee.

Same day registration: No.

Registration deadline (as of Aug 2018): 29 days prior to election.

Online registration: No. Download application form at:

http://www.americansamoaelectionoffice.org/node/7

ARIZONA

(602)542-8683

http://www.azsos.gov/elections

Early voting: Yes. Absentee requires no excuse.

Same day registration: No.

Registration deadline (as of Aug 2018): 28 days prior to election.

Online registration:

https://servicearizona.com/webapp/evoter/selectLanguage

ARKANSAS

(800)482–1127

http://www.sosweb.state.ar.us/elections

Early voting: Yes.

Same day registration: No.

Registration deadline (as of Aug 2018): 30 days prior to election.

Online registration: No. Download application form at: https://www.sos.arkansas.gov/uploads/elections/ArkansasVoterRegis trationApplication.pdf

CALIFORNIA

(800)345–VOTE

http://www.sos.ca.gov/elections

Early voting: Yes. Absentee requires no excuse.

Same day registration: Yes, including on election day.

Registration deadline (as of Aug 2018): 15 days prior to election.

Online registration: https://registertovote.ca.gov/

COLORADO

(303)894–2200

http://www.elections.colorado.gov

Colorado is an all-mail voting state.

Same day registration: Yes, including on election day.

Registration deadline (as of Aug 2018): through election day.

Online registration:

http://www.sos.state.co.us/pubs/elections/vote/VoterHome.html?menuheaders=5

CONNECTICUT

(860)509–6100

http://www.ct.gov/sots

Early voting: No. Excuse required for absentee.

Same day registration: Yes, including on election day.

Registration deadline (as of Aug 2018): through election day.

Online registration:

https://voterregistration.ct.gov/OLVR/welcome.do

DELAWARE

(302)739–4277

https://elections.delaware.gov/index.shtml

Early voting: No. Excuse required for absentee.

Same day registration: No.

Registration deadline (as of Aug 2018): 24 days prior to election.

Online registration:

https://ivote.de.gov/voterlogin.aspx

DISTRICT OF COLUMBIA

(866)DC–VOTES

http://www.dcboee.org

Early voting: Yes. Absentee requires no excuse.

Same day registration: Yes, including on election day.

Registration deadline (as of Aug 2018): 21 days prior to election.

Online registration:

https://www.vote4dc.com/ApplyInstructions/Register

FLORIDA

(866)308–6739

http://election.dos.state.fl.us

Early voting: Yes. Absentee requires no excuse.

Same day registration: No.

Registration deadline (as of Aug 2018): 29 days prior to election.

Online registration:

https://registertovoteflorida.gov/en/Registration/Index

GEORGIA

(404)656–2871

http://www.sos.ga.gov/elections

Early voting: Yes. Absentee requires no excuse.

Same day registration: No.

Registration deadline (as of Aug 2018): 28 days prior to election.

Online registration:

https://registertovote.sos.ga.gov/GAOLVR/welcome.do#no-back-button

GUAM

(671)477–9791

https://gec.guam.gov/index.php/for-voters/for-voters

Early voting: No. Excuse required for absentee.

Same day registration: No.

Registration deadline (as of Aug 2018): 11 days prior to election.

Online registration: Inquire at:

https://gec.guam.gov/index.php/for-voters/for-voters

HAWAII

(808)453–8683

http://hawaii.gov/elections

Early voting: Yes. Absentee requires no excuse.

Same day registration: Yes, including on election day.

Registration deadline (as of Aug 2018): 28 days prior to election (see https://olvr.hawaii.gov/ for information on late registration).

Online registration:

https://olvr.hawaii.gov/

IDAHO

(208)334–2852

http://www.idahovotes.gov

Early voting: Yes. Absentee requires no excuse.

Same day registration: Yes, including on election day.

Registration deadline (as of Aug 2018): If mailed, must be postmarked by the 25th day prior to the election.

Online registration:

https://apps.idahovotes.gov/OnlineVoterRegistration

ILLINOIS

(Springfield) (217)782–4141

(Chicago) (312)814–6440

https://www.elections.il.gov/InfoForVoters.aspx

Early voting: Yes. Absentee requires no excuse.

Same day registration: Yes, including on election day.

Registration deadline (as of Aug 2018): 27 days prior to election for regular registration, 16 days prior for online registration (for the November 2018 general election).

Online registration:

https://ova.elections.il.gov/

INDIANA

(317)232–3939

http://www.in.gov/sos/elections

Early voting: Yes.

Same day registration: No.

Registration deadline (as of Aug 2018): 28 days prior to election

Online registration:

https://indianavoters.in.gov/

IOWA

(888)767–8683

http://www.sos.state.ia.us/elections

Early voting: Yes. Absentee requires no excuse.

Same day registration: Yes, including on election day.

Registration deadline (as of Aug 2018): For people under 18, the pre-registration deadline is 10 days before general elections and 11 days before all other elections.

Online registration:

https://mymvd.iowadot.gov/Account/Login?
ReturnUrl=%2fVoterRegistration

KANSAS

(800)262–8683

http://www.voteks.org/

Early voting: Yes. Absentee requires no excuse.

Same day registration: No.

Registration deadline (as of Aug 2018): 21 days prior to election.

Online registration:

https://www.kdor.ks.gov/Apps/VoterReg/Default.aspx

KENTUCKY

(502)564–3490

http://www.elect.ky.gov

Early voting: No. Excuse required for absentee.

Same day registration: No.

Registration deadline (as of Aug 2018): 28 days prior to election.

Online registration:

https://vrsws.sos.ky.gov/ovrweb/govoteky

LOUISIANA

(800)883–2805

http://www.geauxvote.com

Early voting: Yes.

Same day registration: No.

Registration deadline (as of Aug 2018): 28 days prior to election for registering in-person and by mail. 18 days prior to election for online registration.

Online registration:

https://voterportal.sos.la.gov/VoterRegistration

MAINE

(207)624–7736

http://www.maine.gov/sos/cec/elec

Early voting: Yes. Absentee requires no excuse.

Same day registration: Yes, including on election day.

Registration deadline (as of Aug 2018): 21 days prior to election if registering by mail. There is no deadline if registering in person.

Online registration: No.

MARYLAND

(800)222–8683

http://www.elections.state.md.us

Early voting: Yes. Absentee requires no excuse.

Same day registration: Only during early voting period.

Registration deadline (as of Aug 2018): 21 days prior to election.

Online registration:

https://voterservices.elections.maryland.gov/OnlineVoterRegistratio
n/InstructionsStep1

MASSACHUSETTS

(800)462–8683

http://www.sec.state.ma.us/ele/eleidx.htm

Early voting: Yes.

Same day registration: No.

Registration deadline (as of Aug 2018): 20 days prior to election.

Online registration:

https://www.sec.state.ma.us/OVR/

MICHIGAN

(517)373–2540

http://www.michigan.gov/vote

Early voting: No. Excuse required for absentee.

Same day registration: No.

Registration deadline (as of Aug 2018): 30 days prior to election.

Online registration: No. Download a mail-in registration application
at:

https://www.michigan.gov/documents/MIVoterRegistration_97046_
7.pdf

MINNESOTA

(877)600–8683

http://www.sos.state.mn.us

Early voting: Yes. Absentee requires no excuse.

Same day registration: Yes, including on election day.

Registration deadline (as of Aug 2018): Registration temporarily closes 20 days prior to election, and re-opens on Election Day for voters who register at their polling place.

Online registration:

https://mnvotes.sos.state.mn.us/VoterRegistration/VoterRegistration Main.aspx

MISSISSIPPI

(800)829–6786

http://www.sos.ms.gov/Vote/Pages/default.aspx

Early voting: No. Excuse required for absentee.

Same day registration: Yes, including on election day.

Registration deadline (as of Aug 2018): 29 days prior to election for in-person registrations. 28 days prior (postmark date) prior to election for mail-in applications.

Online registration: No. Download form at:

http://www.sos.ms.gov/Elections-
Voting/Documents/Voter_Registration.pdf

MISSOURI

(800)669–8683

http://www.sos.mo.gov/elections

Early voting: No. Excuse required for absentee.

Same day registration: No.

Registration deadline (as of Aug 2018): 27 days prior to election.

Online registration:

https://s1.sos.mo.gov/votemissouri/request

MONTANA

(888)884–8683

http://sos.mt.gov/elections

Early voting: Yes. Absentee requires no excuse.

Same day registration: Yes, including on election day.

Registration deadline (as of Aug 2018): Regular voter registration closes at 5p.m. 30 days before Election Day for most elections. Individuals can late-register at the county election office beginning the next day and through close of polls on Election Day.

Online registration: No. Download mail-in form at:

https://sosmt.gov/Portals/142/Elections/Documents/Officials/Voter-Registration-Application.pdf

NEBRASKA

(402)471–2555

http://www.sos.ne.gov

Early voting: Yes. Absentee requires no excuse.

Same day registration: No

Registration deadline (as of Aug 2018): The third Friday before the election.

Online registration:

https://www.nebraska.gov/apps-sos-voter-registration/

NEVADA

(775)684–5705

https://nvsos.gov/sos/elections

Early voting: Yes. Absentee requires no excuse.

Same day registration: No.

Registration deadline (as of Aug 2018): Mail-in deadline is 28 days prior to election. Online deadline is 19 days prior to election.

Online registration:

http://www.registertovotenv.gov/

NEW HAMPSHIRE

(603)271–3242

http://sos.nh.gov/Elections.aspx

Early voting: No. Excuse required for absentee.

Same day registration: Yes, including on election day.

Registration deadline (as of Aug 2018): Through election day.

Online registration: No. Apply at your town or city clerk's office, or at the polling place on election day.

NEW JERSEY

(609)292–3760

http://www.njelections.org

Early voting: Yes. Absentee requires no excuse.

Same day registration: No.

Registration deadline (as of Aug 2018): 21 days prior to election.

Online registration: No. Download voter registration forms at:

http://www.njelections.org/voting-information.html#vrf

NEW MEXICO

(800)477–3632

http://www.nmvote.org/

Early voting: Yes. Absentee requires no excuse.

Same day registration: No.

Registration deadline (as of Aug 2018): 28 days prior to election.

Online registration:

https://portal.sos.state.nm.us/OVR/WebPages/InstructionsStep1.aspx

NEW YORK

(800)367–8683

http://www.elections.ny.gov/

Early voting: No. Excuse required for absentee.

Same day registration: No.

Registration deadline (as of Aug 2018): Postmark or hand deliver form at least 25 days prior to election.

Online registration: No. Download application at:

http://www.elections.ny.gov/VotingRegister.html#VoteRegForm

NORTH CAROLINA

(866)522–4723

https://www.ncsbe.gov/Voting-Options/Voting-in-North-Carolina

Early voting: Yes. Absentee requires no excuse.

Same day registration: Only during early voting period.

Registration deadline (as of Aug 2018): 18 days prior to election.

Online registration: No. Download application at:

https://www.ncsbe.gov/Voter-Information/VR-Form

NORTH DAKOTA

(800)352–0867

http://www.nd.gov/sos/electvote

Early voting: Yes. Absentee requires no excuse.

Same day registration: N/A (no registration required to vote).

Registration deadline (as of Aug 2018): N/A (no registration required to vote).

Online registration: N/A (no registration required to vote).

OHIO

(877)767–6446

http://myohiovote.com

Early voting: Yes. Absentee requires no excuse.

Same day registration: No.

Registration deadline (as of Aug 2018): 28 days prior to election.

Online registration:

https://olvr.sos.state.oh.us/

OKLAHOMA

(405)521–2391

https://www.ok.gov/elections/Voter_Info/index.html

Early voting: Yes. Absentee requires no excuse.

Same day registration: No.

Registration deadline (as of Aug 2018): 24 days prior to election.

Online registration: No. Download application at:

https://www.ok.gov/elections/Voter_Info/Register_to_Vote/

OREGON

(503)986–1518

https://sos.oregon.gov/voting/pages/voteinor.aspx

Oregon is an all-mail voting state.

Same day registration: No.

Registration deadline (as of Aug 2018):

Online registration: 21 days prior to election.

https://secure.sos.state.or.us/orestar/vr/register.do?
lang=eng&source=SOS

PENNSYLVANIA

(877)868–3772

http://www.votespa.com

Early voting: No. Excuse required for absentee.

Same day registration: No.

Registration deadline (as of Aug 2018): 28 days prior to election.

Online registration:

https://www.pavoterservices.pa.gov/Pages/VoterRegistrationApplica
tion.aspx

PUERTO RICO

(787)777–8682

http://www.ceepur.org

Early voting: No. Excuse required for absentee.

Same day registration: No.

Registration deadline (as of Aug 2018): 50 days prior to election.

Online registration: No. To register for elections go to the local municipal Permanent Registration Board to fill out the registration form and submit the required documents.

RHODE ISLAND

(401)222–2345

https://vote.sos.ri.gov/

Early voting: No. Excuse required for absentee.

Same day registration: No.

Registration deadline (as of Aug 2018): 30 days prior to election.

Online registration:

https://vote.sos.ri.gov/ovr/?search_type=register

SOUTH CAROLINA

(803)734–9060

http://www.scvotes.org

Early voting: No. Excuse required for absentee.

Same day registration: No.

Registration deadline (as of Aug 2018): Mail-in deadline (postmark) is 28 days prior to election. Online deadline is 30 days prior to election.

Online registration:

https://info.scvotes.sc.gov/eng/ovr/start.aspx

SOUTH DAKOTA

(605)773–3537

https://sdsos.gov/elections-voting/default.aspx

Early voting: Yes. Absentee requires no excuse.

Same day registration: No.

Registration deadline (as of Aug 2018): 15 days prior to election.

Online registration: No. Download form at:

https://sdsos.gov/elections-voting/assets/VoterRegistrationFormFillable.pdf

TENNESSEE

(877)850–4959

http:govotetn.com

Early voting: Yes.

Same day registration: No.

Registration deadline (as of Aug 2018): 30 days prior to election.

Online registration:

https://ovr.govote.tn.gov/

TEXAS

(800)252–8683

http://votetexas.gov

Early voting: Yes.

Same day registration: No.

Registration deadline (as of Aug 2018): In person deadline is 28 days prior to election. Mail-in deadline (postmark) is 30 days prior to election.

Online registration: No. Fill out and print form at:

https://webservices.sos.state.tx.us/vrapp/index.asp

U.S. VIRGIN ISLANDS

St. Croix: (340)773–1021

St. John: (340)776–6535

St. Thomas: (340)774–3107

http://www.vivote.gov

Early voting: No. Excuse required for absentee.

Same day registration: No.

Registration deadline (as of Aug 2018): Not available.

Online registration: No.

UTAH

(800)995–8683

https://secure.utah.gov/voterreg/index.html?fromLocation=

Early voting: Yes. Absentee requires no excuse.

Same day registration: Yes, including on election day.

Registration deadline (as of Aug 2018): 7 days prior to election.

Online registration:

https://secure.utah.gov/voterreg/login.html?selection=REGISTER

VERMONT

(802)828–2464

https://www.dmv.org/vt-vermont/voter-registration.php

Early voting: Yes. Absentee requires no excuse.

Same day registration: Yes, including on election day.

Registration deadline (as of Aug 2018): Through election day.

Online registration:

https://olvr.sec.state.vt.us/

VIRGINIA

(800)552–9745

http://www.sbe.virginia.gov

Early voting: No. Excuse required for absentee.

Same day registration: No.

Registration deadline (as of Aug 2018): 22 days prior to election.

Online registration:

https://vote.elections.virginia.gov/Registration/Eligibility

WASHINGTON

(800)448–4881

http://www.secstate.wa.gov/elections

Washington is an all-mail voting state.

Same day registration: Enacted, but not yet implemented (as of March, 2018).

Registration deadline (as of Aug 2018): Online and mail-in deadline is 29 days prior to election. In-person deadline is 8 days prior to election.

Online registration:

https://weiapplets.sos.wa.gov/MyVoteOLVR/MyVoteOLVR

WEST VIRGINIA

(866)767–8683

https://www.vote.org/state/west-virginia/

Early voting: Yes.

Same day registration: No.

Registration deadline (as of Aug 2018): 21 days prior to election.

Online registration:

https://www.vote.org/register-to-vote/west-virginia/

WISCONSIN

(866)868–3947

https://myvote.wi.gov/en-us/

Early voting: Yes. Absentee requires no excuse.

Same day registration: Yes, including on election day.

Registration deadline (as of Aug 2018): Online and mail-in deadline is 20 days prior to election or at your polling place on Election Day.

Online registration:

https://myvote.wi.gov/en-us/RegisterToVote

WYOMING

(307)777–5860

http://soswy.state.wy.us/elections/elections.aspx

Early voting: Yes. Absentee requires no excuse.

Same day registration: Yes, including on election day.

Registration deadline (as of Aug 2018): Mail-in deadline is 14 days prior to election. You can register at your polling place on Election Day.

Online registration: No. Download application at:

http://soswy.state.wy.us/Forms/Elections/General/VoterRegistrationForm.pdf